Shattering and Bricolage

Shattering and Bricolage

David Bowles

INK
BRUSH
PRESS

ISBN: 978-0-9888632-4-8
Library of Congress Control Number: 2014940550

Manufactured in the United States of America
Cover Art: Nicol Bowles

Ink Brush Press
Temple and Dallas

In Memory of
Martha Maldonado González—
las voces han callado; descansa ya.

Poetry from Ink Brush Press

For information on these and other Ink Brush Press books go to
www.inkbrushpress.com

Acknowledgments

Several of the poems in this collection previously appeared in the following journals and anthologies:

Along the River
Concho River Review
Eye to the Telescope
Gallery
Huizache
Illya's Honey
Interstice
Red River Review
Texas Poetry Review
Twenty

My sincerest thanks go to the editors of those publications for their vote of confidence.

I also want to recognize the vibrant literary scene of deep South Texas, which has given me an opportunity to read many of these pieces in public forums. Specific thanks goes to Edward Vidaurre, the founder of Pasta, Poetry & Vino; Alan Oak, who hosts poetry events in the lower Río Grande Valley; Rachel Vela and We Need Words for their regular readings; Ileana García-Spitz, whose striking photography has documented the blossoming of RGV verse; and Brenda Riojas, whose radio program *Corazón Bilingüe* has become an important space for the literature of the border.

Un abrazo muy grande for the other Valley poets who have been generous with their friendship, advice, feedback and artistic ideas: Julieta Corpus, Erika Garza-Johnson, César de León, Katie Hoerth, Daniel García Ordaz, Lady Mariposa, Christopher Carmona, Octavio Quintanilla, Amalia Ortiz, Vanessa Brown, Alejandro Cabada, Rodney Gómez and all the rest. ¡Raza!

I am also indebted to the generosity, guidance and inspiration of other poets throughout the state: Rosemary Catacalos, Texas Poet Laureate for 2013; Jan Seale, the 2012 Laureate; Karla K. Morton, the 2010 Laureate; Alan Birkelbach, the 2005 Laureate; James Hoggard, the 2000 Laureate; Carmen Tafolla, the first Poet Laureate of San Antonio; Michelle Hartman, Ann Howells and all the rest of the Dallas Poets Community; plus Guadalupe García McCall, Sarah Cortez, Sandra

Cisneros and the dozens of other fine Texas writers whose verse I so deeply admire.

The greats have left their indelible mark on us all, and it seems nearly superfluous to mention them, but I would like to bow my head for a moment before Rumi, Bashō, Dickinson, Whitman, Frost, cummings, Hughes, Plath, Angelou, Borges, Storni, Poe, Baudelaire, Heaney, and all the others who have sustained me in dark times and intensified my joys.

Finally, a few individuals are directly responsible for my deciding to write poetry: my parents, who exposed me to the psalms and ecstatic verse of the Bible and had me stand before congregations to read and sing those rhythms aloud; William Hetrick, my junior high English teacher, who pulled the lid off poetry and showed me the inscrutably beautiful innards; and Lee Hamilton, the professor who taught me the true value of verse as the best tool we have for understanding our place in the cosmos.

CONTENTS

Knowledge

Illusion

Meditation

Devotion

Action

Knowledge

The Smell of Rain

I remember the rain,
Its indifferent pattering a gray counterpoint
To my neighbor's weeping and wheezing.
We were both only seven,
But he begged me
Like a bereaved parent
To help him find his dog.

We combed that cul-de-sac
On our bikes
On foot
On hands and knees.
My own dog Witchy
Had died not six months earlier
And I was driven by the image
Of her broken body
Resting on my lap
As the light left her eyes.

Soaked by drizzle, I braved
The dense hedges
Beside a shut-in's shuttered home.
There, staining the grass
Some malevolent hue,
A small dog's viscera was strewn
In ropes and ribbons and glints of white.

A sob hitched acridly past my clenched teeth,
And I teetered for a moment.
The air, tinged metallic,
Insinuated itself through my sinuses
Into my lungs,
Into my soul.

My knees bent and I crouched,
Overcome.
I saw something stuck fast
To a grate at the foot of the wall—
It was a little dog heart
Thrown clear by whatever vicious attack
Had rent my neighbor's pet to shreds.

Suddenly furious, I seized a fallen branch,
Pried the heart from the grilling,
Tossed it into a hedge,
Scraped the gleaming guts
Into the undergrowth,
Rubbed the slick soles of my sneakers
Along the stain,
Hissing with inexplicable rage.

After a moment, I stepped back,
Chest heaving,
Eyes wide.

No sign of death remained.

My neighbor, his search fruitless,
Called out to me, bereft.
I stepped into the front yard
And confronted the question in his eyes.

"Nothing," I croaked. "Couldn't find him."
He visibly slumped. The lie heavy
On my tongue, I added,
"He probably ran away."

Stooped with resignation, he shambled home,
Brokenhearted, but unbroken,
And my mind swelled with

Terrible understanding
That has never faded

A dark duty that coils rusty
In the secret places of my brain,

Like the smell of rain.

Birdlaw

When a murder of crows encircles the weak,
Their mute, black gaze impassive for eternal seconds
Before talons and beaks deliver swift death—
That is the birdlaw.

When a cuckoo climbs from the shell
To roll those rival eggs from the nest,
Mouth agape for foster-parents' food,
Urging with rapid, cacophonic cries that mimic the brood—
That is the birdlaw.

When a Nazca boobie on the hard Galapagos
Kills her weaker sibling, freshly hatched,
Only to be bitten and pecked by females grown
(Who also wrought sororicides on those bleak beaches)
Violence snarling like a wire in her brain
So she grows to likewise bite and peck and maim the weak—
That is the birdlaw.

When two starlings, having claimed the same breeding site,
Lock feet in mid-air and slash with summer-bronzed beaks,
Raining black-plumed ruin on their mates—
That is the birdlaw.

When a jealous female warbler,
Faced with competition for a single helpful mate,
Sneaks into rivals' nests and smashes their eggs
So that just her fledglings have a sire—
That is the birdlaw.

But when rosella parrots review their young
And find some larger than the rest,
Food is spread with equity,
The eldest chick sharing with the youngest,

The strong with the weak,
Until balance is achieved.
That is the birdlaw as well.

And when weavers in Africa craft their vast colonies,
With room enough for a dozen scores of pairs,
Open to multiple species in commensal peace,
Platform for the nests of even the vulture and the owl,
Teeming and alive for a hundred years,
Generation after generation—
That, too, is the birdlaw.

This River

Threading greengold from distant mountains
ever present, always changing,
endlessly plunging
headfirst into the sea.

Mother and nurturer down the long eons,
she cradles her many children:
Coahuiltecan tribes
hunting and fishing along the sacred sliver of water,
fragile lives that abut the mythical now;
Spanish settlers
hoping for glory, gold or God,
discovering destinies never dreamed;
Americans driven by expansionist vision
to push ever farther into the wilderness,
thinking they have bent this river to their will
when in reality, like all wise mothers,
she merely lets them feel they have control.

She holds us close in her watershed,
Among currents, recodos, vast reservoirs,
Through basins, bosques, deserts, fields
Whispering green dreams into our infant minds
Before nestling us on a sandbar at the delta's edge.

Seasons in the Valley
a haiku sequence

The dry brush crackles,
wilts feverish, awaiting
those tresses of flame.

Blood-warm Gulf waters
spin out clouds, frenzied by the
sun's languid embrace.

Storm clouds form a wall;
a skein of lightning cracks bright
and makes it tumble.

Summer shade, trembling,
watching for her father's car—
film-inspired kiss.

Dog days of summer
that growl and sink white fangs deep
into November.

A northern storm of
white hair and Bermuda shorts:
winter has arrived.

The temperature dips
to a cozy sixty-five.
Old men sigh, content.

Twenty-eight degrees—
farmers coat their trees with ice;
school is cancelled quick.

Dew clings tenacious
to the windshield, shrugging off
insistent wipers.

The mall parking lot,
replete with Mexican plates:
it's finally spring.

From a Balcony above Santa Cruz Bay

Oaxacan flânerie

Boats moored along a cobbled wharf,
Flashes of white and cornflower blue
Against a calm, dimpled green
Broken by the glassy wake
Of a tour that's reached its end,
All ringed by buildings stuccoed pale
And topped with rusty clay,
Palm-wreathed and dappled bright.

To the west, the foothills of the Sierra Sur
Rise, thickly timbered: just a fleeting glimpse
At the shy road that coils silent,
Unobtrusive.

To the south, the bay—
Small strip of sand almost hidden
By vegetation, stippled with bodies
Like blobs of blurry color
That hint at a shape more distance
Will gradually reveal.

Jagging past into the deepening blue
Like a broad and holy path to the bosom
Of Chalchiuhtlicue, foam-flecked goddess
Of the depths, the wind-scoured pier sits
On sturdy cement pylons
Sunk into watery shadows.

Beyond, boats ply with stately calm
Waterways that hug jutting,
Wooded beachheads,
Growing smaller, more indistinct,
Less mechanical, unrecognizable

As they approach the vast Pacific,
Which stretches endlessly,
Shading mystical gray
Before becoming
Sky.

Emptiness

Thus taught the master:
Constant practice. Learn all forms.
Once they are mastered,
empty yourself of technique,
of desire to control.

Then, when the time comes,
art itself will move your hands
spontaneously,
your body a conduit
for the universe's will.

Andromache's Prayer

Silent Andromache kneels in the shadows of Troy's walls—gutted,
Smoldering bastions of lost hope, death and degenerate hungers—
Patting the mound of indifferent sand, the widow, unheard, weeps.
Under her hand lies Troy's sad destiny, shield's curve cradling,
Wrenched from his mother as uncles and grandsire had been as well,
Noble Astyanax, prince of the city that Argives have murdered.

One above others Andromache curses: Achilles, the butcher,
Father and brothers' assassin, the slayer of Hector her husband,
Sire of the villain who flung from the walls the innocent baby
Buried today (shade winging its way to Elysian Fields, yes:
Priam and Hector awaiting him). "Neoptolemus: *New War*.
Bastard's own name is a key to his nature," Andromache mutters.

"Me? I'm *War among Men*," she reflects with a hushed sob, pensive.

Standing, she lets tears dry on her face, looks sullenly seaward:
Slave to him now, lone son of Achilles, aglow by the black ships,
Gesturing haughtily, Helen and Sparta's old king in his shadow
Lengthening ominously toward dead Troy now as Helios drops low.
"Doubtlessly talking of marriage, those three; will Hermione shudder,
Feeling those bloodstained hands on her? Gods, will you keep me from
      screaming?"

White-armed Helen appears to be laughing, but Hector's new widow
Hates not Zeus's fair daughter; Andromache knows in her heart's core
Wars are not fought for the noble excuses, the specious incentives
Men claim angrily spur them. The truth is the Argives have come for
Glory and gold and the raping of women, their only true gods Death,
Eros and War. To the last of these three now Andromache bows down:

"Hated Lord Ares, you bringer of slaughter, I yield you my one son.

Chomp his white corpse greedily—hurled from Troy's heights—
Calm your hunger, Widower, briefly: soon more
Babies you may anxiously make us give you:
Quench now your red thirst . . .

May you choke on his blameless flesh, you sick fiend!"

And she spits her libation out on hot sand.

Bussokusekika

There in the driveway,
two sets of little footprints—
my enlightenment.
Eroding shapes remind me
that everything is fleeting,
even the love of a child.

The Swirling Black

a han-kasen renga

As blue-spangled skies
deepen over bleak vistas,
comes the Swirling Black.

A man scrabbles on tip-toe,
reaching for his autumn noose.

Axes tilt, worlds plunge
into gelid barrenness,
scoured free of all life.

Prophets who lead their people
into the maws of terror.

A black sewer rat,
its wiry fur infested
with bubonic fleas.

Asteroids pummel the Earth,
extinguishing every life.

Hot, withering gusts
spark hungry, rising-red flames
that gnaw at the woods.

As she squeezes dry her breasts,
a woman mourns the unknown.

At galactic cores
apocalyptic monsters
wreak cosmic havoc:

The primal power they yield
will soon annihilate them.

A boy lies in darkness:
stark, deadly epiphanies
cause him to tremble.

Ovens crackle with the sound
of burning human gristle.

A gaunt silhouette
half-dead in the morning cold
strikes one final match.

Here stands an empty city:
its people died of famine.

Galaxies collide
whole civilizations wiped out
in quantum madness.

Thrust deeply into despair,
a father slaughters his sons.

Divine minds awaken:
though they struggle to impose
eternal order,

The Swirling Black spirals down
to close their eyes forever.

Puhahabitu

The People knew about the truth
In ways we only vaguely see;
No man can point it out to us
No priest retains the needed keys.
Its power dwells where each believes
That truth resides; to reach its strength
There's nothing you can really do:
The more you strive to grasp at truth
The further truth will move from you.

The People said you must lie down for power,
You pick a place where someone blessed with truth
Has spent much time, or even died, and there
You wait. And pray or meditate. And wait.
In silence contemplate while opening yourself.
And then, not God some local source of power
May choose to pity you and gift you with a truth
That's tailored to your needs, with special songs to sing,
Or other amulets to help you wield
The mighty tool for living well you've gained.

Perhaps you won't be answered.
Perhaps you'll die of hunger.
Perhaps you'll choose a sterile site
Where charlatans have seemed to draw
A power that was only feigned.
But if it is truth you would have—
Real power, truth, or "medicine"
(As puha is so sadly called)—
You must lie down for yours,
And stop trying to steal ours.

Rhyme Ran to Rap

Rhyme ran to rap
nudged roughly by Milton,
slanting along Dickinson's tongue,
taking the road less traveled
by smug-faced, black-clad elitists.

Rhyme ran to rap,
hustling through the Harlem Renaissance,
tapping her feet to bluesy, gospel-soaked jazz
while chanting hymns
in blessed stupor.

Rhyme ran to rap,
skipping rope and laying the dozens
on beatniks and hippies
who smirked at her childish antics
'cause poesy ain't music.

Rhyme ran to rap
on platform shoes,
spinning vinyl late into the night,
climbing with funky steps
that Sugar Hill.

Rhyme ran to rap,
and danced for a time
on a hustler's lap
then slung billingsgate
at sucker emcees;
grabbed guns, aimed straight
for luck's bum knee;
stuttered thundering from the lips of thugs;
slipped fluttering down breasts, hips and bums
till she evolved into a dreadlocked muse

who inspired bards of all creeds and hues
to embark on a lyrical hero's trek
that could lift their gifts from the streets and protect
the legacy of the human race,
preserved in words that can't be erased
because their sounds burrow deep in every mind
encoding our struggle in a weft of rhyme.

Cretan Glance

In me flow two disparate streams
Whose fountainhead is human history.
Though I've tried to dam one's course,
Their waters smash through every dike.

The darker stems from parts unknown
Heady and warm like Dionysian wine;
My self gets lost, smashed in its rapids,
My consciousness and soul erode.

The lighter stream is ordered logic,
Objective truth through rational thought:
Dispassionate, yet filled with beauty:
Apollonian mind rejects the banal.

"Take on the mind of Christ," some say.
"You are small and your spirit is sinful."
The East says that self is but illusion,
And we suffer until we learn to let go.

Empiricists coolly affirm that truth
Is found through deliberate, conscious research;
Then they prove that there is no self,
No consciousness and no free will.

Constantly creeping toward some goal,
The Combatant takes leaps upward.
A trillion memes, whirling endlessly,
Push apeman toward uncertain futures.
God evolves, and I still strive for apotheosis.

With the poise of Kazantzakis
I look on life with a Cretan Glance,
Standing in the absence that makes me a man,
A dervish on the edge of the abyss.

From the contradictions arises a third eye:
Darkness and light are annealed in my heart.

I stared the bull down:
Never ran nor was I gored.
I joyfully faced the eternal void,
An atheist in love with God.

Both drunken priest of dark woods
And pilgrim pastor on his knees,
I exist though I know I don't:
I seize life with enlightened grunt.

I look on life with a Cretan Glance:
A dervish on the edge of the abyss.

Identity

I come from groping blind processes in primordial dark,
From gradual expansion that moves toward complexity.
I come from glacial cerebralization, ever larger, ever deeper,
Folding in on itself in layers of slow awakening
(Sensing first food, then the others, then danger, then—
Ever so achingly slowly—the self).

I come from the very first *I*, the AUM of nascent sentience,
        from the very first words hoarsely grunted on the savannah.
I come from flint and stone and spear and bone, a thousand
        small technologies passed mouth to mouth and mind to mind.
I come from story, STORY, the human mind mirroring the universe
        and longing to understand and becoming part of the story it tells.

I'm from boats that crossed into the Arabian Peninsula,
        a tribe made restless by knowledge, spreading like a vast web
        along the Indian and Asian coast, into Australia, across Europe.
I'm from a species that supplanted Neanderthals because those cousins
        had no language, no story, no infant culture gestating divinity.

Nomads and farmers, priests and kings, merchants and soldiers
        and scholars, mothers and queens, priestesses and prostitutes—
Tents and towns and stone cities with towering walls, ziggurats and
        earthen mounds, ploughs and wagons, logs and hempen ropes—
Mesopotamian libraries and laws, Brahman born on Ganges' shores,
        analects and koans and sutras and suras and psalms, warbling
        chants on twilight shores—traditions of beats, melodies, drones.

And always the mind, searching and testing, prodding and projecting.
I am the discipline it made for itself: deduction and hypothesis and test.
I discard my *self* for a better mask.
I am the knowledge picked piece by piece
From the cryptic encoded cosmos,
Then rebuilt in our brains, in our books,

In our hard drives, through our nets,
Our new appendages of silicon and steel, reaching out into the world
        and tweaking, restructuring, recoding, improving,
Till I, and you, and all of us have the universe at our fingertips,
And we merge with it,
And become all.

Musashi's Way of Knowledge

The ronin gave his students
nine principles of learning.

Clear your mind of lies—
think of what is right and true:
make it your mantra.

Whatever you choose to learn,
practice its every skill.

But do not exclude
the arts, so vital to life.
Study them as well.

Grasp the underlying truth,
the principles that govern.

Everything can harm
as well as help. See the whole
essence of the world.

Your gaze must be accurate—
do not turn away: look hard.

Not all truths are clear:
delve beneath the obvious
to find the hidden.

Take great care in all you do,
even what seems not to count.

When you choose to act
after long consideration,
do nothing useless.
Let these principles guide you,
and all knowledge can be yours.

Three Mythic Deaths

I. Green Woman

The young border patrol agent shakes his head in silent anger
As his older partner empties his pistol into the water,
Laughing at the screams of retreating immigrants.

His grandmother once told him legends of the Matlalcihua,
The Green Woman, spirit of the river, nourishing mother.
Indignant, he growls a secret prayer to her attendants:
Trickster elementals, chaneques long dormant, who now awaken.

Reeds twine round the shooter's legs;
The mud quickens, sucks at his feet.
And glowing green the current streams into the air,
Plunging like a waterfall to drown him where he stands.

II. The Owl Calls

Two women, drunk, in the parking lot of the Cypress Lounge,
Their ears still ringing from the raucous
Rockabilly band.

As they laugh, full of love and life, an owl passes overhead
The tecolote bajeño, also called the aurora, harbinger of death.
It creaks a desolate, ominous cry:
"Teckoorus cuckoo! Teckoorus cuckoo!"

A harrowed glance exchanged as two bottles shatter on the blacktop.
Whose soul is it calling?

The singer, stepping out for a smoke, finds their corpses hand-in-hand.

III. Mexican Vampire

The screech owl flits in through the open window,
Alights on the headboard.
Tilting its head, it regards the baby curled against its mother's curves.
Its round, glowing eyes blink once, twice.

With a shudder it stretches and morphs,
Feathers becoming hair, wings arms.
The bare breasts and buttocks of a woman rest beside the infant
(She's left her legs behind to better fly through the night),
And she dips her mouth to that smooth, innocent skin,
Cooing as she drinks deep.

In the morning, covered with bruises, the little corpse is cold.
Wailing parents, steeped in tradition, spur the village to revenge.

The Ghost of the Moon

The ghost of the moon
Trembles upon the river,
Its pallor cracked and veined
By the oblique shadows of branches—
Ebony and mesquite, grasping at darkness.

Like a lunar fragment
A white form floats in those mangling waters
A face obscured by spidering hair and giant reed,
A lifeless hand, caught in the thirsty roots
Of brush holly,
Scarlet beans like globules of blood
Afloat in the black.

Nativity

First the inchoate gesture, the pantomime primeval,
eyes that follow, hands that mimic:
slow aggregate of skills down the millennia.

Then the syllable, a grunt of exertion,
of surprise, of contentment, repeated
as part of the process, ritualized.

And the rhythm, echoing the endless heart,
the pulsing blood, the pounding surf,
the rushing flood, pluvial pizzicati on broad leaves.

Accompanied after an age by the melody,
stolen from the birds, a burble on dumb lips,
ululation in rough throats, like the wind through hollow logs.

And gradually, the rise of the symbol:
the sound standing in place of the thing,
first where it's present, then where it's not.

Soon a swarm of tokens, spoken singly
or very seldom run together, beads drilled
and strung in the air, tremulous constructions,

Till order arises, recursion like a map of eternity,
subordination a foretaste of sharper and sharper eyes
that will peer into the fabric of the universe.

Now the long, steady labor of compilation:
glittering webs in the mind that trap data
and impose strange new order on the world.

Story is born, first the halting biography
and then a gleeful glut of gossip that gives rise
to speculation and unabashed fiction.

The swirling mirrors of the mind reflect the webs
so the soul in abiogenesis congeals within connections.
Apocalypse or savior, Homo Sapiens emerges, blossoming.

The Lost Verses of Nezahualcoyotl

I. Doubt

From birth I was told to look Beyond,
To the warrior's glory that awaits me—
Eternity spent winging my way cross the sky,
A companion of the life-bringing sun,
Or resting beside the cosmic sea
In the shade of the world tree
In that Eastern paradise where stands
The House of Holy Writ.

In my youth, the priests and my father the king
Taught me the noble way—
Just as the gods let their blood be spilled
To set the sun in motion,
So valiant sacrifice is required
Of man, woman and child.

But years in exile nourished my doubts,
A dark and fearful time—
What if all that exists is *this*,
A brutal, empty life?
What if when we are shorn of our flesh
Nothing there awaits?

My comrades and brothers and fellow philosophers
Rejoice in the thought of reunion
As butterflies, hummingbirds, mighty ghosts
There in the House of the Sun.
And I so desperately want to believe:
I listen to the earth and air,
Straining to hear the thrumming voice
Of the Giver of Life,
Searching for a tangible bridge

To that Unknowable Realm.
But what if all that exists is *this*,
If all we have is *now*?

I strive to make Texcoco great,
Surround myself with beauty,
Craft auspicious systems of law,
Finance, justice, art—
Convoke the greatest Nahua minds
Remake the very hills
While composing these bittersweet songs,
These fleeting flowers of the heart.

They will one day wilt and wither;
Texcoco will be no more;
Acolhuans and Mexica will disappear,
Their kings at last forgotten;
This fifth and final sun will die,
Like every sun before—
But for a moment we laughed in its light,
Like wind-blown petals
Sparkling near an exile's campfire
Before the flames take them.

II. Tollan

Listen, Itzcoatl, Mexica king:

The ancient songs relate the dream
Of wise and gentle Quetzalcoatl—
Lord of Tollan, legendary city.
After seven years upon the mountains
Doing penance for his sins,
His own blood drawn in holy rites,
The youth fell deep into a trance.

The sacred mother, Tonantzin,
Appeared to him in a vision.
"My dearest son," she whispered soft,
"Remember who you are."
And as he reached to touch her face,
Drops of blood spattered the ground—
Each bloomed into a star,
The earth became the sky,
And Quetzalcoatl burned bright like the sun.

In the dream, birds and butterflies
Threw themselves upon a fire
While men and women pricked their flesh
To draw a single tear of blood,
Singing as they squeezed it into the flames.
In the heavens, the future king of Tollan
Felt his body swell with energy,
Fed by the praise and selflessness
He witnessed there below him,
A vast field of flowers, yearning toward him.

This was his epiphany, my dearest friend—
Once he had fought and won his nation back,
He proscribed all human sacrifice,
Found better ways to nourish the sun.
For this he is revered and loved
All across our varied land.

You who would join all Nahuas as one,
Think on his example. Do not burn
The sacred painted books of history.
Do not veil the past with lies.
Remember that the sun continued on its way
Passing each day over Tollan
Though not a soul was slain.

In Mexico, your word is law.
If you choose the darker path,
I will not interfere. I will stand by you.
But in Texcoco, as long as I rule,
We will remember the dream
Of our Feathered Lord,
And weep to know ourselves fallen.

Illusion

Cemetery

The soft whirring of the chain, muffled crunch of tread on gravel—
Spanish oaks, gnarled and stooped with age,
Lean across the empty lane, mossy beards tumbling
In tangles that almost brush my troubled head.
My eyes scan the overhanging branches for black rat snakes
As the glooming deepens, tingeing my thoughts an ashen grey.

Beyond the old trees, the swamp teems obscurely,
Its coarse thrumming voice a welcome countermelody
For my own inner plainsong. I imagine alligators
Moving with lethargic deliberateness,
Cottonmouths slicing through murky water,
Converging on the lone teenager
Who has wandered away from the land of men
To trespass in the realm of the Red Queen,
Tooth and claw and buzzing rot.

To the cautionary croaking of sentinel bullfrogs,
I arrive at the vine-choked walls of a Civil War cemetery.
Shedding my bike like a withered carapace,
I drift through the entrance, under that crumbling arch,
To be greeted by a scarlet sea:
Crumbling tombstones, overgrown with Virginia creepers
Rubbed bloody by autumn's ruthless touch.

On my knees before a granite cross worn nearly blank
By the passing years—as I would fain efface myself,
Erode into the fetid green—I gather a handful of purple berries,
Plump with tangy poison. Death will come slow,
Like a beautiful girl who does not turn away,
But presses her bony frame against mine, robbing my heat.

A twitter, bright and alive, conspicuous in this twilight—
A mockingbird quirks her head at me a few yards off,
Perched upon a huckleberry bush. She sings again,
One of a hundred songs she knows, a bemused melody
That dispels the gloom against my crooked will.
I let my escape dribble to the leaf-coated weeds,
Walk to the auspicious plant, yank some blue spheres free,
And resignedly sink my teeth
Into shuddering sweetness.

Deep Blue Bottomless Soul

"[L]ulled into such an opium-like listlessness of vacant, unconscious reverie is this absent-minded youth by the blending cadence of waves with thoughts, that at last he loses his identity; takes the mystic ocean at his feet for the visible image of that deep, blue, bottomless soul, pervading mankind and nature; and every strange, half-seen, gliding, beautiful thing that eludes him; every dimly-discovered, uprising fin of some undiscernible form, seems to him the embodiment of those elusive thoughts that only people the soul by continually flitting through it. In this enchanted mood, thy spirit ebbs away to whence it came; becomes diffused through time and space."

—Herman Melville, *Moby Dick*

Enigmatic gam on the foam:
Not quite spirit, not just bone;
Flotsam beach and jetsam shore—
Leeward breakers crash and moan.

Empirical compass, sounding pole
Shivered my mast, stove my soul.
Dog-vane flutters on a spar,
But the sail is furled upon the yard.

Drop my eyes to white-capped sea
Cast wide my net . . .
My net is me—
Deep blue
Bottomless soul.

Alone, on the brink of the watery abyss, the vast void which gapes incomprehensibly wide on every side of me, I stare into its unsoundable depths, despairing at understanding aught but my own reflection, broken like a pinwheel upon its foamy surface. Clenching teeth against rising bile, with wet eyes I search for the pale forms that move glacially beyond the glassy mask, hoping for and yet dreading that Leviathan that comes to drag me deep.

From fathoms down now comes a roar;
Should slip the cable, head for shore,
But my mind has yawed from all that's sane,
For I've learned the secrets of the brain.

Ghostly bulk cracks inky blue,
Mottled white—a frightening hue.
The beast arises from the sea
And turns his milky gaze on me.

I stare with horror at his eye:
I'm not reflected . . . only sky.

Who am I?
Do I exist?
No . . . I . . . I don't know!

It opens wide its maw for me:
I cannot turn, I cannot flee.
Bone-white teeth and pitch-black throat—
I slowly lower from the boat.

Oblivion I now embrace,
My self's façade I shall efface.
Like Jonah once, I see I'm naught;
I dive within the dark I've sought.

The whale plunges, sounding deeper and deeper, past all clinquant, filtered
light, to the unknowable darkness thousands of leagues below human ken.
And there, on the verge of mighty molten rivers and geothermic vents and
pressures that should crush the very marrow from my bones ... it releases
me, and I ... still ... am.

Deep blue
Bottomless soul
Here below
It's beautiful.

I am here
Amidst the blue;
I always was,
And so were you.

The flitting forms,
They are the soul
We are the sea;
We are the Whole.

Here below
It's beautiful.
I am here,
And so are you.

Tatuajes y Placazos

Tabula rasa walls and flesh loom
Amidst tintinnabular, clustered squirm.
Costumed selves, unaware they've masked the soul,
Surge impotent against vast faceless hell,
Made ephemeral by the few famous:
Initiates who arrogate a voice.

Creeping toward the blankness of brick and skin,
Clutching needles, ink and eloquent spray cans,
They defy anonymity and
Trace the whorls of their selves in the wind:
Tatooed and graffitied glyphs that combine
In a defiant, life-affirming skein—
A fleeting rainbow that twists in the air
And proclaims, "We existed. We were here."

Vizier

You would have me build a temple
To the false gods of your freedom,
And you'd exorcize the daimons
Who plant scripture in my mind.

How you long to play the tyrant,
To watch peons bow and scrape
As if power and position
Could at last erase your shame!

All those years impoverished, humbled,
Spent in fields and meager shacks,
Climbing slowly from the mire—
They twisted your soul, but never mine.

So I'd rather hold you captive
In the chains of my achievements
To growl hoarsely like a vizier
In the imam's wiser ear.

Nagual Tragedy

The wolf,
its eyes aglow,
is chased through moonlit brush
by mounted men, machetes raised
to kill
       the beast.
It stops and shifts
into a boy who warns
of demon dogs. Heedless, they swing
their blades.

For hours
they scour the scrub
for more *naguales*—men
who don the skin of animals—
find none.
        At home
there is slaughter:
woman and children dead.
Black dogs await. The men, wailing,
retreat.

Hell hounds,
undaunted, snarl.
But bursting from the dark,
white wolves attack and slay the dogs.
survivors weep,
ashamed.
        With grunts
wolves shed their skins.
Nude, men grasp spades. Bereft
husbands, fathers, stand by their sides
and dig.

Primal Primates Saw Alkaloid Angels

Primal primates saw alkaloid angels,
perhaps in umbrella fungus
springing from their own warm feces
and therefore from themselves,
maybe even kicking them into
the treacherous realm of consciousness,
initiating ego.

Hominid-kind said, "Let there be god,"
and collectively projected him into
the enigmatic sky
attributing to him the power
to create and destroy,
never realizing it was their own distorted reflection
to which they bowed.

Flayed

I am a beast
In the skin of a man.
Decades past,
I flensed the flesh from a teen,
Fed his guts and ghost
To despair, that blind leviathan.

I do not feel as humans feel—
My beetle brain has other hungers—
But I can pose and mimic and sell
My feigned humanity to son and daughters,
Wife and colleagues: I earn their goodwill
With a smile from a mouth that emptily twitters.

Beneath the dead man's guise
This worm trembles, yearning for humanity
But knowing itself base.
How could I ever deserve love? An obscenity
Like me, which only knows how to use,
Has no place in that community.

It's odd to think
As the years pass, I have learned to pretend
So well that I'm human and not a rank,
Vile monster that most consider me kind
And wise. No one has tried to debunk
The charade, peer past the rind.

This skin has rotted in spots,
Gone leathery where it bears the sun's glare.
I can't say that it actually fits—
Something's changing in me that makes it tear,
Like I'm evolving, growing in sudden spurts,
Ready to split this shell and take to the air.

And though I'm a fiend, I feel hope unfold—
Perhaps my new form will be wondrous and gold.

Keeping It Real

During the 80s I lived in the projects,
Section 8 housing, a block of apartments
Facing the Pharr Community Center.
Dad had abandoned us. I was sixteen,
Sleeping on pallets with Matthew and Thom
(Beds were a luxury Mom couldn't afford).
Grandpa eventually took pity on us,
But I remember that floor and those roaches,
Shouts not quite muffled by paper-thin walls,
Exiting early each weekday morning to
Catch a school bus with roundabout routes,
Arriving in time for a meager breakfast, then
Classes with teachers who didn't pick up on my
Situation, who assumed the güero was fine.
Stuffing my face with government lunch, I'd
Steal to the library, hide there for hours,
Buried in different, preferable worlds.

Determined not to piss off the gangsters, I
Tried to stay out of their way.
Long-haired rocker that I was—
Mostly white, with tattered jeans—
Conflict was certain, near preordained.
Locker doors and I became close friends,
Wanksters kicked and tripped and named me
Joto, pendejo, güero cacahuatero.
Finally, they followed me home to the "hood,"
Knocked books from my hands, laughed as I ran.
That was all. I think they pitied me.

Weeks later, crashing glass from downstairs.
Mom blocked the door, locking us in.
Next morning, a curtain fluttered unhindered
Signaling peace between shards of glass.

Bloody and stark, impressed in the windshield
Of our neighbor's Chevy Nova was the
Shape of some poor bastard's face.
Baby-daddy'd come home and found Sancho busy.

Later that same year, my little brother
Found a dead body in the grass by the
Canal near Ridge Road and Jackson
A teacher with AIDS, whose lovers had killed him.
"Screw this," I finally spat at the cosmos.
"I'm out of this jungle, this ghetto, this hood."
Scraping and learning and working my ass off,
Leaning on others, like the woman I married,
Slowly I clawed my way out of hell.

How do I keep it real, little homies?
My past makes me humble, it keeps me honest,
But I won't retain much more than these memories.
Squalor, betrayal, violence and hunger:
I refuse to believe that these are virtues.
Reality is what we build for ourselves,
Hand-in-hand with our loved ones and friends.
That's the identity to which I am true,
Finding poor souls who are somewhat like me,
Helping them fashion a different world.

The Naked Gnostic Nun

Love stains her mouth with greed;
She trembles beneath the weight of ecstasy and revelation.
She wants to melt the synapses of the world mind,
On her knees muttering abracadabras
To the god of the flesh,
The drunken hairy horny lord of the womb, the void,
The nothing that she discovers herself in
After having licked her magic stamp
And mailed herself right the hell out
Of the irreality of the real.

Her priest says *amen*
And pockets the cash,
Leaving her alone in the throne room
With her reflection in the mirror
And the rotted tree of life on fire
Beside the iron pyrite street outside.

Ebullition

For 20 years their passion slowly waned,
But cooling coals still warm their children's hearts,
So they live like friends and ignore the trend.

But he's so focused on his precious art
He squanders money that his family needs
And doesn't understand his partner's hurt.

She set aside her dreams to raise the kids
And guide her husband to the heights she deserves
To be scaling herself. She's beat the odds,

Though: now his name is quite respected. Hers,
Of course, remains unknown. If anything,
She seems a mousy housewife: mild or worse.

Each passing year drags its cruel claws along,
Scoring deep the chasm that has opened
Between them, freeing underworld bubbling

And vitriolic feelings that will end
This weak charade like magma through a vent.

Beautiful

Look away. I wish you didn't see me like this.
If I could but peel back my ugly flesh
to show you the glowing, ineffable thing
that yearns for you in silent agony...
but here I sit, a gnomish troll,
growing older,
ashamed before your dark eyes.

Would I were beautiful.
Would I had silken wings with which to enfold you.
Brilliant colors with which to enthrall you.
Cherubic songs with which to lull you
into an illusory world
where decades fall away
and form is mutable
and without feeling disgusted at myself
I become worthy of your touch.

Owl, Mockingbird and Crow
after Ted Hughes

Owl had Mockingbird cornered.
He was about to silence her song forever
So his harrowing screech would have no peer.

But Crow . . . Crow turned Owl's screech
Into an insolent raspberry,
And even God laughed to hear the sound.
Owl, humiliated, abandoned his prey.

Then Crow heard the Mockingbird sing
And her voice filled him with wonder.
He wanted that voice,
He imagined his caw transformed:
He would sing himself such marvelous songs!

So Crow tried to pluck Mockingbird's voice from her throat,
But the wound was too deep,
And her weeping blood filled the world,
And her voice hung limply in Crow's beak,
Damaged and silent.

So the screech was gone
And so were the songs.

All that was left was the blood,
Crow's hoarse cawing,
And God's laughter.

Crawling

The gray clouds stretch above
Like grave clothes tight around the world;
The wind has stilled and nothing moves
Except the tears of a wounded girl.

Deep thunder makes me bend
In mute submission to my fate;
She waits for me to stand and fight
But I know it's much too late.

She turns to go,
The rain is falling,
The world has pushed me to my knees,
And now I'm crawling.

Through ash-white, choking mud
I drag myself against the storm;
I've lost it all, I've nothing left,
There's just this shell, this empty form.

For I was just a man,
And how can men face down the dark?
It's forced into their very souls
By the cosmos, cold and stark.

She won't return:
I'm hoarse with calling.
The hand of fate has slapped me down,
And now I'm crawling.

I'm crawling,
But there's nowhere to go,
Just a void outside,
And a void within.

The Orange Embers of Our Dreams

a revolutionary hymn for conquered extraterrestrials

Behold us now the fire has died:
The few your weapons left to weep;
Our homes are cracked, the mud all dried,
Our young ones sleep eternal sleep.

So this is the world you'd make of ours:
Civilized, human, Christian, dead
You mocked our clinging to rock and mire
And plunged us into shit instead.

Embattled peons, broken, true:
Here on the shattered field we stand;
Together now we chant our rue
In deepening shadows, hand in hand.

We face our doom by the light that gleams—
The orange embers of our dreams.

Dark Blot

Strange how such a small dark blot
On so thin a rectangle of film
Should so easily wrench open the sluices of despair.
I hold it to the light, squinting,
My heart already absent from my chest,
A fledging fled before the forest burns.

You rasp some weak assertion,
Your normal boldness drained
Like a drought-stricken lake
By innervating possibilities.
I hear the word abortion
And my mind tilts off its axis.

Water on the brain. An absurd phrase,
Not nearly ominous enough.
Hydrocephalus—the Latin weighs heavy,
Like the arcane pronouncements
Of a judge or priest, the thundering decree
Of an imperious divinity.

I insist on a second opinion,
Even as you flip through a medical text
You picked up at the library,
Moaning like a mother already bereft
When you see those bulging skulls,
Those empty eyes.

Termination. You're adamant. Resolute.
A childhood spent as a schizophrenic's sister
Has robbed you of the will, the compassion,
To raise such a shattered child. Or perhaps
You know a compassion I can't, an existential
Love that halts suffering before it begins.

When we learn the baby is fine,
That its umbilical cord passes over its head
Like the twining dastar of a pious Sikh,
First relief creeps into our eyes, then guilt.
We never could've done it, we assure each other.
But we know. We know what we are.

Balance

Spanish priests arrived,
With tales of God and Devil,
We nodded sagely, smiling.

Devil? Suspended from branches
Of the World Tree, our lives sway
In bewildering balance:

Star demons watch us.

These tzitzimime
Protect women, give men life
Until an eclipse—

Then they drop to devour us.

Herdthink

Pod of thugs fluking downstreet
Drone choreography, communal crime
Want of volition yet complex behavior
Visible hive, but where's the queen mind?
Inaudible echoes that steer the school?
Which the systems that cybernate blind?

Surging mobs that flood the squares;
Angry eddies and crescent waves
Spouting forward, unawares,
To break with vengeance on a man.
Pseudopodia rip and tear
Conscience lost till it disbands.

Geometry of the selfish herd,
Trusting the center, moving as one.
The stock market rises, the stock market falls,
Marching in tandem to some single drum.
Digital Maoism, worldwide collective,
The multitude unthinkingly thrums.

Such relief to lose your identity—
Just herdthink and safely graze.

Watching the polls and flocking with glee;
Kids checking the hands raised to see how to vote.
Relative ease of the sheeples' lives—
Why bother with logic when you learn by rote?
Spacious bandwagon invitingly cruises
Break free of the pattern, you're rocking the boat.

Faith of our Fathers, but not of our hearts:
We worship the most popular god of the day.
We're proud of traits beyond our control

Race, culture and nation define our souls.
Free your unique ego, escape that harm,
Forge individual thought, outside the swarm.

I Wish I Could Remember

I wish I could remember
That *Planet of the Apes* mask
You wore one Halloween.

Or those weird drawings you hung
On the fridge: tongue-lolling beasts
That scared me and made me laugh.

Your pancakes and tortillas,
All in the shape of Texas,
Refusing to be rounded.

When you permed your thinning hair
And all the church members said
You looked like a black pastor.

The way a guitar would sing,
Cradled in those beefy hands
That moved with unearthly skill.

The roiling brown depths behind
Smeared lenses, sparkling
Darkly even when you smiled.

That rich bass rumble, reading
Tolkien, Burroughs, and Bible:
Guiding me through those gardens.

Fishing, hunting, building fires:
Your exasperated grunts
At a son who would not learn.

I wish I could remember
You thus, but all has faded
Except the sight of your back
As you turned away from me,
Leaving forever.

Meditation

In Xochitl, in Cuicatl

I feel an energy surge within
An electric shudder that runs along my nerves
And caroms through my cranium
Growing weightier as it impacts with memories.

Could it be teotl that glimmers in my mind,
That divine spark that Aztec philosophers
Claimed was the ground of the very universe?

I wish I could give a name to this semi-divine outburst
That rushes up, uncontainable,
An alien song that is nonetheless mine,
Escaping from fingers I no longer recognize,
Transformed into words that I never pronounced
But that, instead, pronounce my being:
Syllables of man and flower and god,
Fleetingly united.

Craft

Sometimes I'm a thief,
Sneaking into the House of Holy Writ,
Cracking open dusty tomes,
Breaking thick wax seals,
Rolling open ancient scrolls,
Stealing those heavenly lexemes,
Jotting down furtive phrases
Before slipping guilty
Back into my benighted life.

Sometimes I'm an explorer,
Plying vast, amorphous seas
Of primal thought,
Anchoring at dark atolls,
Scanning alien constellations,
Scrying sluggish sargassoes
That undulate like the torpid tresses
Of naiads and sirens
For visceral, unspoken truths.

Sometimes I'm a wanderer,
Lost in trackless deserts
Of shifting, homogenous past,
Falling for every empty mirage,
Foolishly avoiding each oasis,
Till I stumble onto the ruins
Of long-abandoned monuments
Lifted in na‹vet, by some forgotten me.
I make rubbings of opaque glyphs
And hope to decipher my own dead tongue.

Sometimes I'm a hunter,
Pursuing multi-syllabic prey
Across savannahs, through dense jungles,

Glimpsing mottled hides
As they sleekly leap and blur
Amidst the undergrowth and vines.
With luck I finally corner one
And send my bolt whizzing home,
Only to display the prize like a taxidermist,
All vital magic drained away.

Sometimes, though, I'm a child at play
Beneath the autumn trees,
And, oh! the leaves that scatter down
Upon my youthful head:
Reds and golds and burnished browns,
Piling higher and higher
Till, laughing, I can hold back no more
And I dive into drifts
Of perfect words.

Nine Neo Gnostic Mantras

I. Dictionary Anti-Dialectic

is caste metempiricism?
dissentiate
eat naval princess
drink gemeliparous cilia,
bell sliminess, and my lost labial.

your driver sleep the tack film
a blot halogenous.
spanker of bearer
enfeebler fusible
rue plan poecilitic.

II. Genuflection

dead mountain Moses
call it anything honey-filled
recognize falsely lip left
drawn out desert and thread,
blue or green, into stagnation.

promises always had been
never will be hand-held.
kiwis her fruit coagulated
an unlikely prescience
assembling thereby
and fulfillment shattering
his trip of waterfall.

III. Rehash

a jingle like tambourine ineffable
danceful joy 'round picture jigged

verdant light doors open in obvious invitation
and letters carefully writ.
a gut-whisper dripping
of hormone-tingle confusion
and nipple-gorged snacktime.

tongue-flick meditation
in fleshy spirals you dream green.

IV. Dopamine Diatribe

steaming? get thought.
freedom plots at my gouging of broken identity chunks,
malodorous pressing: got to love windmill flesh.

mind fragmentation ominously large
in scorching of thought, carnivorous
tangle of cryptic absence of "here."
large lips pursed, sucking my valley into this beast,
this son of synapses I've hidden.

vacuum into father
more "out! out with man!"
future war and mass rape:
a this-is-it breakdown.

V. Irreconciliation

furloughed double entente
in grayish metempsychotic lipservice.
was he digging too deep
or no depth peroxide?

but heartlurch unboundless binds
and never breaking free he spits
at shrinking away a priori of advancement,

a don't-really-care self-inveiglement:
the diametric duo rides again.

VI. *Again Polygraphing the Existential Bordello*

an eighth unconsciousness exited
the psychoid nether regions
of waiting room stasis
and metempsychosed into a female fetus.

staring through hazy amniotic ocean
at wombwalls
it feels memories slipping
into 90% prison.

and it kicks a futile kick: einai kai me einai.

VII. *Beschleunigungsspannung Maximal*

full-fledged ptochocracy of society schizogenic
and its idiotypic communism,
rattling into antigenteelness
(which hitherto was regarded as drivel
till snorted quite effectively and
printed enigmatically onto littress intemerate).

lah-dee-dah
whoopdeescatologypeepeedoodoo [mere intensation].

hoary whores lean against doors
and whisper blowjob quotes.
there is no church,
just a keraunograph.

the annihilation of man sabe bien rico,
kind of like strawberry yogurt with M&Ms.

VIII. Experienced Spigot Paean

lilting tilted
I watch it all pour out of me:
infinite amounts of liquid
for you alone to imbibe.

your thirst never sated
as I slowly drip to stop.

IX. Cold-blooded and Coefficient

alas, poor Yorick!
Strunk and White have licked you clean!
stripping you of a thin layer of grime
and rotting tissue
replacing it with shellac and a top hat
like every other skull in Uncle Sam's closet!

Intinction

I'm dipping my mind in the flow of the Vishnus,
Avatars of complex, enduring confection,
These gods of the word, everlasting encryption,
Divinely virtual.

And Krishna has come to amazing existence,
My mind has unzipped the memetic infection:
He's born in my brain, and I spring from his essence,
We cycle endlessly.

Winged Words

A divine fiat hurled from Olympian heights
Or chthonic verdict blasted from nether grottoes
The wind rushes howling down the street
And the newspaper woman shrieks in panic
Stumbling away from cars to weight the bundles down
But in a whirl of typeset chaos and colored inserts
Hundreds of Sunday editions explode into startled flight
Diving amid church-abandoning traffic
Whipping along between pedestrians' arching legs
Hurrying dumbly somewhere, monochrome dodoes
Called by silent, ineluctable, inhuman forces
Streaming through the overcast sky
To crumple themselves useless
In abandoned, illiterate lots
Stands of mesquite trees
Twitching flocks of print
Words destined for
No eyes at
All.

Dancefloor Thrall

Percussive showers spatter feet,
Concussive lights and swirling beat.
Arms uplifted, eyes shut tight,
With stuttered groans she owns the night.

Ravishing the endless void
Though its avatar, every dancing boy;
Ascetic caught in mystic trance,
She's found the truth in primal dance.

Her soul strains at the primordial call:
Sudorific rapture, dancefloor thrall.

Crackling waves of enlightening sound,
Shaman chants now pound and pound;
Her moistened curves conduct and glow:
Frenetic zazen, Dionysian flow.

The spinning turn now makes her burn;
For loss of self she fully yearns.
Mind shuts down, heart opens wide
To let the universe pour inside.

The beat strips her soul free of its caul:
Sudorific rapture, dancefloor thrall.

> "It's simply spiritual.
> Dancing is beautiful.
> I love clubs; they're like temples—
> Deeply spiritual.
> Dancing is so transcendental—
> It's utterly spiritual."

Billowed smoke, thick and white:
Chiaroscuro of shadowed light.
Strobes that morph her very form . . .
More than human, Brahman-born.

The DJ spins his eucharists
As her body wildly arcs and twists;
Far beyond mere meditation
She reaches transubstantiation.

Eight Koans of Rishi Brahmavid

First Koan

Once two disciples—
Rahul and Nanda—
Found Rishi Brahmavid in his study.

"Teach us to see what we are—
Pull us from illusion's mire!"

To the tall man he spoke: "You are Rahul.
And you," he said to the short, "are Nanda."

"But Master, you're wrong!" replied the taller.
"I am Nanda, sir, and that one's Rahul."

Rishi returned to his books.
He said nothing more.
After a while, the two left.

Second Koan

Svetayavari found him on his knees,
Praying in the garden shade.

"But Master," she cried,
Appalled at this devotion,
"There still is no god!"

Rishi simply smiled.
"I'm an expectant father
Crooning to his unborn son."

Third Koan

Rishi Brahmavid
Brought a chimpanzee
To the dining table.

"Serve your brother food,"
He said to his disciples.
The ape smiled at them.

Fourth Koan

An older disciple was complaining:
"The world was so much better
When I was a child."

Rishi Brahmavid slapped him.

Fifth Koan

Rishi's son Gandharva
Refused to study math.

"Mathematics will be the true language of god,"
Said Rishi and sang a song in that tongue.

Sixth Koan

"How do I start on
The true Dharma path?"
A young man asked him.

"Admit you don't exist," said the master.

Seventh Koan

Pratyadeza
Came upon Rishi
Arranging flowers.

"How can I best see Brahman?"
She asked the busy teacher.

He picked up a vase
And tossed it aside.
It burst asunder
Upon the hard floor.

"When you shatter your false self,
Then you'll truly see Brahman."

Pratyadeza
Did not understand.

Rishi added this:
"The air within that old vase
Was the same as that without."

Eighth Koan

Once some religious leaders
Visited Rishi.

Imams, rabbis, priests,
Nambudiri, bhikkuni—
All wanting to test the sage.

"You teach blasphemy,"
They rebuked him with one voice.
"God made man, who strayed

And became corrupt;
What was once perfect
Turned sinful and weak,
Slowly declining.
Soon man will die out."

Rishi wept like one bereaved.
The leaders were stunned.

"What a sad tale, my brothers,
And one so tragically wrong.
You've got it backward:
Man evolved through time.
At first an instinctual beast,
He grew stronger and more pure,
Slowly ascending,
Bursting his boundaries,
Overcoming corruption.
One day he'll make god."

They scoffed at the master's words.

Zazen

Lotus-borne, silent, still
Unfocused without fighting stimuli
She contemplates the unanswerable.

The paradox of existence
Tumbles across the wilderness
Of her emptied mind.

She sees her identity for what it is:
Illusory, accidental, uncontrolled—
A barrier falsely dividing this from that.

Breathing steady, one by one
She relinquishes her greedy grip
On the lines that moor her
To this movie-lot façade.

She sends her soul spinning toward the truth
And prays the impact will shatter her fragile persona,
So that like a glazier she can mount the remains in cames,
Transforming those shards into a glasswork
Through which knowledge will more brilliantly shine.

Monanacahuia

After days of fasting to purify the soul,
The old ones ground the mushrooms down,
Making a coarse flour they mixed with honey
And ate delicately, reverentially.

Then came the chocolate—hot, spicy,
Sipped at all through the long, dark night
As the tunnels of heaven opened wider
And the voices of the gods came swirling.

Some would dance to celestial rhythms,
Crowded round by ghostly forms;
Others wept to see that distant shore
Where the World Tree branches into canopy.

A few, cowering before the looming immensity
That lies beyond the heavens, that starless void
In which primal forces surge and squirm,
Were driven mad by the vision and took their own lives.

But many saw the flowers and feathers fall
In ribboned streams from the Mother's hands
And nodding their heads in silent response
They sat raptly, contemplating eternity.

I Did Not Go to Work Today

I did not go to work today.
I stayed in bed, wrapped in blankets
and a fast-paced, action-packed book.

Then I sat outside with a cup of joe
and watched the cats chase the dog round and round
while sunlight and breeze had their way with me.

I emptied myself of every care,
sat in the bath for half an hour,
dressed in my rattiest jeans and shirt.

I drove alone to the cinema,
bought a ticket for a tearjerker,
wept and rejoiced at the gimmicky tale.

I did not speak a word.
I did not check my mail.
I did not watch the news.

I listened to pulsing techno tunes,
white noise that kept the illusion at bay,
and I doodled random mandalas

Till I found myself so far from my*self*
That I knew there was no going back,
Not to the person I had been that morning.

The wind creaked in the eaves.
The universe breathed,
And I breathed with it.

Yardwork

a mondōka

Slicing through the verge,
I impose my rote pattern
on your chaos as I dream.

Ah, but your order
arises from me, small man,
and my weeds invade your thoughts.

You Are Not What You Seem to Be

You are not what you seem to be—
That happenstance persona
Accreted down the years
Is a mask that blurs the soul.

You are not your nation.
Did you elect to be born there?
Were you involved in its founding?
Its traditions . . . are they your doing?

Nor are you that city,
That football team,
That political party,
That genre of music.

You are not your religion.
I suspect it was passed on to you
Like a family heirloom—
Dusty and meaningless.

You are not your ethnicity,
No matter what joy it brings,
No matter how much sense
It appears to make of the world.

You are not your race, either,
Though the limited personae around you
Would love souls to be that simple,
Would love to facilely explain you away.

Nor are you that tattoo,
Carved by another into your flesh,
Making life-long the ephemeral.
Not surgeries. Not ever-dead hair.

Merely materials, waiting for order,
Purposeful mosaic, reshaping.
Shrug off the accidental self—
You are not what you seem to be.

You are a swirling flock of symbols
That began nesting on the day of your birth
In the dense branches of your brain,
But you've allowed one pattern to dominate.

And if I could just convince you to let them fly
Unchecked, unhindered, in formless whorls,
A universe of wonder would open up
And you would find your source.

Devotion

Master of the Board

His nimble fingers snatch godlike at a bishop,
Foil my gambit with a single flick.
Smiling at me, he mutters a clever quip.
He's only twelve, but it's not beginner's luck.

So much of me in him, twined with his mother's wit,
Her audaciousness, her eye for pattern.
I marvel at the balance as he grins. "Checkmate,
Dad. Sorry. You're tired. Maybe if we play again . . ."

Oh, wonderful boy, I want to cry,
You beat me fair, you bested your dad.
Don't apologize for your amazing mind.
I'm proud to call you master of the board.

But we are also friends. Rivals. Men.
So with a grin I gather my fallen pawns,
Line them up uselessly before king and queen.
"Okay, you uppity punk." I laugh. "It's on."

A Boy's Heart

A boy's heart
Yearning for freedom,
For vast open spaces
Yawning beneath a bright expanse of stars.

Yearning for solitude
Courageous rebellion,
The right to stand alone,
To strive against the cosmos with head held high.

Rejecting civilization,
Its tinctures and paints,
All the rigid vestments
That immobilize the coursing blood.

Rejecting every rule
Enacted to curb the speech,
The inchoate passions, the unbridled joy
Of boyish dreams.

Wanting to capture beauty
Or craft it with agile hands,
Not to *be* beautiful,
Nor remade to fit some prized ideal.

Wanting to choose, unhindered,
The path into paradise or perdition,
Flying through the whirlwind wild
Or lumbering over ice-gnawed peaks,
But always in movement—
Never yielding,
Never caged.

I hear its rhythm, wondrous child,
And I sense your puzzled fear,
For you've a boy's heart, yes,
Blundering and blessed—
But it beats within a woman's breast.

Mother Earth

Bedrock hard, you've become the foundation
On which we each erect our lives,
Bearing the weight of our dreams and disasters
With broad footings that spread across the naked stone.

Like some antediluvian goddess,
Drawn and quartered by patriarchal hungers
You've become the very earth, your essence spread
To nourish children and mate, to give us rest.

You push with the painful persistence
Of glacial geology, tectonic friction,
And up rise islands, snow-clad mountains
That thrust us toward the stars.

Can we draw you skyward,
Lift your iron heart into the heights?
Should we sacrifice some elevation
To bear you, too, aloft with us?

We must, I think. We'll fashion anchors
From your rebar-veined cement
To keep us from drifting aimlessly,
All ballast abandoned, into oblivion.

Philotes

Across the miles I feel your joy
For friendship spins its unseen threads
From heart to heart to bind us all;
Though distance pull them taut and thin,
It cannot truly sever them.

They form a web of strength and love
That sometimes, in our darkest hour,
Will glow with supernatural light
To guide us swiftly through the night
Back to the waiting arms of hope.

Becoming

I drop the hypospray.
Nanocells course through my body,
Then await, quiescent.

I peer at you across the lab,
Distant and silent as ever.

"So what would you have me become?
A woman, like her, tall and haughty
Like a surrogate mother? Or perhaps
The womb isn't important to you.
Shall I become a t-girl, lank and lean,
With perky breasts and a secret prize?
Ah, it's just a different sort of man
You're waiting for, isn't it?
Tell me. I am nothing unless you will it."

You say nothing for a while, then
Your lips part finally, cracked and dry.
"I want . . . I want you to be *me*," you whisper.

I nod, swallow hard. Your DNA is ready,
The helices dancing virtually in the system.
I trigger the command. The nanocells begin.

Pain doubles me over. Bones stretch. Muscle
thickens, broadening my chest. My lose robe
Bubbles and flutters as my flesh melts, reforms.
My member lengthens, its foreskin reborn.
The world quavers around me, new angles,
And I cry out, stumbling.

You catch me,
Your mouth finds itself, your tongue probes
Its yearned-for twin. Your arms are about you,
Four hands that tremulously rip away barriers—
And you rejoice finally to love and be loved.

Prayer to a Mackerel Plucked from the Sea

Sleek, glistening, dark,
Meat compact beneath crystalline scales,
You are pulled into this boat
As the Pacific rocks us silent.

Forgive the deception, the bright colors
That drew you to the ineluctable bite of pain
Now fading in your mouth
As you start to die.

My children's eyes are downcast—
They have not learned to face your awful, precious gift.
They do not see the honor in your moribund dance,
Unbearable honor that must be borne.

Behold their tears, salty drops
From that primal sea whence you and I
And all of us emerge at last, my brother,
To feast or be feasted upon.

So I tell them
To intone with me
This prayer
Of thanksgiving:

> We take your life
> So we may live.
> Not out of greed
> But so we can feed.
> Not because we can
> But because we must.

We see you, brother,
And honor your sacrifice
Without guiltless packaging—
We see you for what you are
And accept ourselves as well.

Making a Man

Just as Quetzalcoatl, for a fifth time,
Stubbornly resolved to make mankind,
Descending into the netherworld
To face the Lord and Lady of Death
And steal from them the bones
Of all his failed attempts,
Then returned with that broken ivory
To Tamoanchan, flowery realm of the gods,
So the Mother of All could grind them to flour
And mix them with drops of holy blood
Shed by her divine children,
Kneading humanity into existence—

So do I swear to struggle once more,
To scour this hell for the shattered skeleton
Of our troth, regardless of the cost to me.
When I return to you sometimes goddess,
Sometimes demon, always loved
Promise me you'll pulverize the past,
And I'll let my veins run dry
So that you can mix a mortar
With which to shape a better man.

Adamant or Silk

There she stands in unseen splendor,
Emanating gradual light.
Shadows flit, her image bends,
Wavering on the very verge.

Blinking eyes to clear the vision,
Haunted by her shimmering shape.
Hands outstretched defy all doubt
And find her limbs so firm and warm.

Adamant or silk she moves,
Burgeoning and beckoning;
Adamant or silk she proves,
Trusting without reckoning;
Adamant or silken grooves
Of flesh and souls and heaven strings.

and the mind's afire

Bones and thews like metal struts:
Her muscle sheets are laid so thin.
But oh! how soft those curves can roll
Like water flowing over jade.

Her angles leave the deepest cuts
Like scythes that pass through verdant glades.
The wisps of smoke now couple, hungry:
She's joining granite with mirage.

Adamant or silk she flies,
Burgeoning and beckoning;
Adamant or silk she cries,
Trusting without reckoning;

Adamant or silken sighs
That set the steel to trembling.

and the mind's afire

Ruby Red

Transplanted, grafted, pruned—
The ruby red thickens greenly
Between irrigation trenches,
Tended and fertilized by able hands
With the unwavering devotion of a father.

For years it yields up sweet, pink flesh—
Sticky pulp that fairly bursts from the rind
In gladsome sacrifice. Proud stands that tree,
Weathering hurricanes and drought,
Coated with ice to survive a freeze.

But the orchard keeper grows old, dies—
His sons divvy up the acres, sell them quick,
And the ruby red feels the mute screams
Of its brethren, felled with sudden violence,
Tenacious roots prised from soil like dead fingers.

Alone, the grapefruit tree survives for a time—
Its leaves yellow like a jaundiced child,
Its proffered globes bear strange, stigmatic scars,
And they drop unpicked to burst upon the ground
(The newcomers shudder at the taste of that sacred shaddock).

Inexorably the leaf-cutter ants encroach—
One cool spring night the winged ones
Spiral through moonless dark in nuptial flight
And fertile queens land to establish new colonies,
Crescent mounds of loose, rich, fungal earth.

With no one to beat back the horde
The ruby red soon teems with black specks
And trails of green-parasoled workers network out
Across the weed-choked dirt, past the frame house,
Down into the inscrutable earth.

Leaf and bark, fruit and bloom—all devoured.
Starved, gnawed to its core, the tree dries to kindling.
Oblivious owners experience a small spasm of regret—
How much a bag of that hybrid fruit would have fetched!
Shrugging, they snap off sun-bleached branches to add flavor
To the slabs of meat sizzling on the immolating grill.

Stewardship

The meaning of life?
Objective morality?
Simply stewardship.

Stewards of this earth
to which life and wisdom cling,
joeys on her back—

Not because she is fragile,
but for duty's sake
and because she is mother.

Stewards of sentience,
rising behind beastly eyes
that peer at wonders

Like hominids, long ago,
faced the awesome sky,
lost without a sibling guide.

Stewards of each soul,
spiraling unique, kludged selves,
kaleidoscopic beauty—

Nodes of a vast, unseen web
on which hard-won lore
thrums and thrives and evolves.

Stewards of knowledge—
ever expanding,
deeper, wider, more complex—

Trembling as we comprehend
the power it brings
to destroy all that we love
or save the vast, doomed cosmos.

Bhakti

The wind's own son examines, bites and breaks the gift
His orange eyes, they peer at every stone he plucks,
And Rama, angered, tries to understand his friend.

"'Tis worthless, Lord: the bracelet bears not your sigil,"
Hanuman says. The demon Vibhishana mocks:
"Why not destroy your flesh as well? It too is plain."

Devotion questioned, brave Hanuman doesn't flinch.
The monkey pulls his flesh aside to show his love
For carved in every bone is Ram's holy name.

I read this teary-eyed, and something bubbles deep.
My inward-turning vision scans the porous white,
But not a word is written, nowhere lurks a god.

A sigh: I'd guessed as much, but whimsically I sink
To cells, to chromosomes, to codons, genes
Obsessed increasingly by dumb, unknown desire.

I enter molecules and burrow deeper still,
Near drunk with hope, but growing sad with every void,
Approach a proton, pry it desperately apart

Unleash the quarks and bosons, quantum bits of stuff,
And in a maddened thrash of deepening despair
I find your name, aglow in every particle.

Tonantzin

Her form at repose, lying on one side,
Hands clasped in a careless mudra,
Sleep relaxing her features,
Smoothing the lines of age
So that mother and bride and child
Seem to exist simultaneously.

Did husbands and children
Upon distant savannahs,
Campfire sparks dissolving
Into stars above them,
Look upon their own women thus
And yearn for a vast maternal embrace?

Curled upon the warm earth,
Hearts brimming with sudden love,
Did they feel the slow, steady heartbeat
That thrums beneath us all the days of our lives,
Geological rumblings like vibrant shakti,
A mute but beautiful lullaby?

For motherhood is creation of life,
And who but a goddess could stir blind cells
To tremulous, awestruck awareness?
Therefore, let even the agnostic patriarchs
Of fire-speckled, icy darkness
Utter a prayer to that warm, tangible divine.

Action

Beyond Mirando City

for Jan Seale

There are places where the stricken world tapers to an end:
Thin spots, bereft of voice or birds,
From which obscure vehicles in endless caravan siphon
Essential mysteries or dark green dreams.

I'd not stop at such blighted corners of creation,
But life draws one close at times,
To contemplate the bloated spiders and dust
Amidst crumbling gray stones.

Once I chanced upon what seemed the edge,
Last border 'twixt here and gone,
A hapless town of curtains and rusted cars,
White glare, long black shadows.

In the company of a kindred soul I stopped,
Both unsure we'd have another chance
To refresh before we risked the lip of the world:
Mirando City, leagues from Laredo.

In a weed-choked park we cringed, obeisant
To vast, empty, blue-spangled sky,
And forsaking ablutions or curtsies or smiles,
We set off to crest that final hill.

Somehow we knew the gap is bridged by words,
So we twirled garlands of songs, jests, quotes,
Bits of half-remembered verse, epiphanies:
Lovely, ascetic detritus of literate lives.

Laughing, we flung our flowery grapnels
And swung 'cross that chasm deep,
Mind-to-mind in the sempiterne dark,
Glittering with writ, lore and wit.

We emerged at last beyond Mirando City
To the beautiful rattle of kingfisher cries,
And awestruck I saw the edge must exist
So that we twist garlands together.

Belonging

As awareness blossomed,
I learned I was an outsider.
Abandoned kinder (I could already read),
Spent much of first in third-grade classes,
Forever labeled oddity.

At least I belonged to my family . . .
Yet year by year they grew stranger—
Or perhaps they did not grow at all.
Our bonds, increasingly frangible,
Stretched, shuddered, snapped:

I was left unmoored.

In high school, my small karass
Gelled out of nowhere—
Ron, Gus and I, tight philotic web
Of poverty, exclusion and books,
Bountiful books,
Hardy, welcoming scriptures
From Nabokov to Stephen King
In which we found belonging.

But time and college and girls
Frayed those ties, too,
Till I drifted through sargassoes
Of drink and agnostic night,
Alone.

Then my anchor finally snagged a kindred soul,
An outsider likewise adrift,
And in a hospital room,
Amidst antiseptic fumes
That will forever remind me of paradise,
We found a way to forever belong,
Led by little, grasping, wrinkled hands.

Upcycled

Out back, a tower of shipping pallets:
Tottering empty, utility ended.
Face blank, she flips one off the top,
Watches it hit the matted grass.

She's arranged her tools and paint nearby:
She hefts a smallish sledge hammer
With grace—those slender fingers and wrist
Swing the weight like dancer's frappé.

Spine snapped, the pallet yields
To her crowbar's constant prise and pull.
In minutes, a stack of weathered boards
Rises in its place, pitted by nail holes.

And now the magic begins. Look:
Her eyes narrow. She measures, jigsaws.
The compressor throttles to life, hissing,
And slat upon slat is nail-gunned into place.

In what seems merely minutes, a chair stands,
Sturdy and comfortable, perfectly angled.
Under her sure hands, its surfaces grow smooth,
Glow like a costly hardwood antique.

A click and puff of changing hoses,
And paint settles evenly across its planes.
One can almost imagine the wood's joyous cry,
Upcycled from rubbish to handcrafted beauty.

A Young Brujo Learns the Mystery

A town in southern Mexico
Some centuries ago was home
To a clan of wise sorcerers
For whom magic was a sacred tool.

The youngest boy, he came of age;
Apprenticed to his grandfather,
He plunged into holy energies
Both within his heart and without.

He learned the hieroglyphs that glow
In tree and rock and flowing stream,
The language of the animals,
To don the jaguar's spotted hide.

He practiced songs that call the rain,
The gestures that drive evil off,
And mixed the ancient herbs that heal
The maladies of heart and soul.

One day, now sure of his control
The boy alone surveyed the stones
Inscribed with spells beyond his ken,
The jars replete with potions dark.

His pride caused him to try a hex
To bend a young heart to his will,
A village girl with golden eyes
That never deigned to glance his way.

But on the morrow there she sat
Oblivious to his desire,
And in a rage the boy rushed home
With curses in his heart of hearts.

His anger curdled in those jars
And as he broke into the room
They shuddered before his bleak rage
And shattered in a million shards.

In tears, the boy cried out ashamed,
"¡Abuelo, ven! I've done great wrong!"
His grandfather came and surveyed
The destruction with saddened eyes.

The young brujo told him what he'd done,
His desire for the pretty girl,
His fury at his failed attempt,
The tragedy that then ensued.

In quiet tones the man replied,
"Verás, m'ijo: we mages learn
That greed and rage serve no one but
Tezcatlipoca, Lord of Ruin.

"For centuries that bitter god
Has sought to bind this universe
In chaos and darkness and hate.
But the Feathered One resists.

"Quetzalcoatl. It's him we serve.
We strive to create, to balance,
To heal every wound that we find.
And therein lies the greatest secret."

Closing his eyes, the old man knelt,
Reached out his hands and gathered shards,
Fitting piece against piece, guided
Only by a spiritual sight.

Dumbstruck, the boy watched those fingers
Form the image of a smiling girl.
The old man stood. Some shards remained,
Too damaged to be used again.

"Here is the mystery, m'ijo:
The jars are forever broken,
Something has been truly lost, but
In its place new beauty arises.

"You see, my boy, the Lord of Ruin . . .
He does not seem to understand.
Though love and order he'd negate,
Each shattering brings a chance to create."

The Gatekeeper

Without fail he slips in at four,
glancing furtively over his shoulder,
shuffling quickly to the fiction section
to pull the next book from the shelf.

The librarian's heart aches for him,
small for his age, poorly dressed,
hungry for shelter, surcease, escape.

Over the weeks she draws him out,
uses his love of fantasy and sci-fi
to engage him, guiding him to classics
from the Golden Age, which he devours.

He lives, she learns, in government housing
just down the street, apartments teeming
with gangsters and mothers' boyfriends.

To him the library is a sacred refuge,
a sanctuary replete with silence,
cool shadowy niches,
the smell of paper.

School ends and he spends days entire
in the library, his meditative breathing
punctuated by the rustle of turning pages.

She uses his interests as a segue, a lure,
and he follows her into books of science
and history, discovering the rainbow
bridge into actual past and plausible future.

One day the young man does not return.
Nor the next. Nor ever again. Gone.
He is not the first. He will not be the last.

But she will continue to guide them, hoping
they remember the path to the secret gate,
the one she helped them find, there
among her library's meager stacks.

Hurricane and the Basilisks

Wrapped in the cooling mists of early creation,
Hurricane and Feathered Snake wandered the world,
Inspecting all they had made.

The animals gaped and bowed their heads
As the bright-plumed serpent swooped
'Twixt heaven and earth, at home in sea or sky.

While Hurricane, all swirling black,
Made hills flatten in fear, trees bend in awe:
He roared his might and bared his lightning grin.

But the animals loved Feathered Snake,
Dreamed of nestling beneath his broad wings,
Safe amid all that red and green and blue.

Envy snarled in Hurricane's heart—
The beasts were equally his, shaped by his winds,
His power roiling in their guts and glands.

He spoke not a word to Feathered Snake,
But in deep chasms of the earth set to work
Crafting a twisted echo of the ally he despised.

Strange eggs he formed, and set black vipers
To wrap themselves around the leathery shells
Till these hatched, spilling forth basilisks.

Each winged serpent, motley riot of color,
Hissed its way off to the kingdom of beasts,
A misshapen mockery of Feathered Snake.

Lulling the animals into a loving stupor,
Each cockatrice would envelope its prey
In a vicious, deadly embrace,

Winging the tremulous soul to Hurricane's
Dark whirlwind maw, to be consumed
Eternally, its fear sheer bliss for the fiend.

Too late to help, Feathered Snake learned of the slaughter.
His heart was shattered by the suffering of his beasts.
He looked on Hurricane and bowed his head.

"Release them now, brother, friend. Let them live.
What is it you wish of them? Of me? No unchecked
Massacres. You and I should be in balance."

Hurricane split in a rictus of electric blue.
"Worship is all I crave, foolish bird. While you
Flitter about, they have hope, and do not fear me."

"Strike me, then. Set me alight. Immolate my quetzal plumes.
But release the animals, friend. Let them tremble back
To horrified life beneath your swirling black."

So Hurricane struck. Aflame, Feathered Snake took to the sky.
The souls streamed free, bodies breathed in ragged snatches.
Basilisks hissed while their master thundered with laughter.

Still higher he flew, the flaming bird, past the glowing mists
Of that primal age, climbing the sky, brighter and brighter
Til he became the sun, bathing the world in his light.

The basilisks shrieked and burrowed deep, seeking relief.
And Hurricane understood with a howl of rage
As the beasts basked in the warmth of that first day

That every creature might bend its knee to his wrath
But he could not crush the hope they felt
And they would never, ever love him.

In the Dark

How was it you knew
when you reached out in the dark
that I was willing?
My flesh still bears the hot brand
of your touch, scarred and fading.

Toward a Mexican Bakery

It's 35 degrees and drizzling gray
As I dart along a street
In San Nicolás de los Garza
Beneath a borrowed umbrella,
Searching for sweet bread.

Dancing away from puddles
And mud-slurry splashes,
I scan the endless rows of buildings
Patchworked together, none of a piece,
A riot of color and seams and wire.

The cold has sunk its fangs into my flesh:
I hunch over to retain some heat
As the whistling tramontane
Tugs at my clothes with eager fingers,
And I grunt a bitter curse.

The other pedestrians glance at me—
We share chagrined smiles.
What choice have we,
Driven by a need for broken bread
And steaming drink?

Kintsukuroi

Like a hammer deliberate
Or careless, jostling child,
Life tumbles us
From safe, oblivious heights
To smash to shards
And scattering dust.

Yet, though shattered,
We may have the fortune
To feel warm, compassionate hands
Collect the fragile fragments
Of our broken selves.

With care that glitters brighter
Than even the purest gold,
They join the misshapen bits together
Leaving a webbing fretwork
Of shimmering seams
That forever remind us—

When wounds are healed by love,
The scars are beautiful.

Shattering and Bricolage

Expand through shattering and bricolage:
When self becomes a barrier to soul,
You must remake yourself as a collage.

Instead of building walls 'gainst the barrage
Of thoughts and data that you can't control,
Expand through shattering and bricolage.

Identity is simply a mirage:
Accepting you're a fragment of a whole,
You must remake yourself as a collage.

Each human being is but a blind montage,
So while they wait for you to play your role
Expand through shattering and bricolage.

Shake off the reins, the cultural dressage,
For when you make enlightenment your goal
You must remake yourself as a collage.

Come join me in memetic sabotage:
Let's crack the masks society would mold!
Expand through shattering and bricolage:
You must make yourself as a collage.

He Was Going to Change the World

a chōka for would-be saviors

History conspired,
bringing every element
together in him
needed for a messiah.

So it felt to him,
broken by life and remade
into something more:
a vessel of cosmic truth.

Then he got married.
He loved his wife very much,
but she did not heed
his profound revelations.

Then children were born—
they clung to social norms,
refused the protests,
their father's revolutions.

His friends smiled and laughed:
he was a good guy, they said,
just a bit obsessed.
Should loosen up and have fun.

At last he despaired
of ever changing the world
and focused inward
on being the best he could.

To his great surprise,
he glanced around at his life
and found he'd changed what mattered.

Huckleberry Juju

a Southern tanka sequence

Swamp folk are singing
of huckleberry juju
and magnolia fire—
bayou flatboat drifts along
beneath a palmetto moon.

Broom by the doorway
Till fowl crow at last arrives—
by silver starlight
a root doctor's searching out
the boo-hag's secret shanty.

The sun rises bright,
and the early morning wind
brings the marshland smells
up dusty streets to my porch,
sets granny's swing to swaying.

The day of the Lord—
choose gospel elevation
at a backwoods church
or Gullah conversation
with the smiling hoodoo man.

Weave sweetgrass baskets,
teach the children to catch sense—
on these coastal isles
frayed brotherhood is mended
through simple taking of hands.

Sip some sun-brewed tea,
barbecued squirrel on the grill.
Stir that Frogmore stew
and the lucky Hoppin' John
could use a slice of cornbread.

A sweet southern belle,
with her pigtails and cornrows,
sits on your knee, friend—
Go take a roll in the hay,
Feed her fresh huckleberries.

Kids fish in the ditch
with bologna on a string
for crawdads and toads
while a gator cools his blood
in the noisome chocolate mud.

Blacksnake is napping
high up in a mossy oak.
Baying in the swamp,
hounds are tracking a raccoon
through a cottonmouth rainstorm.

Sun sets red and white,
tongues of magnolia fire
that flicker and fade,
while twilight spreads thick and blue
like huckleberry juju.

www.ingramcontent.com/pod-product-compliance
Lightning Source LLC
Chambersburg PA
CBHW022011090426

42741CB00007B/987